Science In Your Life:
ELECTRICITY
Turn It On!

Wendy Sadler

Raintree

www.raintreepublishers.co.uk
Visit our website to find out more information about **Raintree** books.

To order:
☎ Phone 44 (0) 1865 888112
🖹 Send a fax to 44 (0) 1865 314091
💻 Visit the Raintree bookshop at **www.raintreepublishers.co.uk** to browse our catalogue and order online.

First published in Great Britain by Raintree, Halley Court, Jordan Hill, Oxford OX2 8EJ, part of Harcourt Education.
Raintree is a registered trademark of Harcourt Education Ltd.

Editorial: Melanie Copland, Kate Buckingham, and Lucy Beevor
Design: Victoria Bevan
and Bridge Creative Services Ltd
Picture Research: Hannah Taylor
and Catherine Bevan
Production: Duncan Gilbert

Originated by Chroma Graphics (Overseas) Pte. Ltd
Printed and bound in China by
South China Printing Company

ISBN 1 844 43658 6
10 09 08 07 06
10 9 8 7 6 5 4 3 2 1

British Library Cataloguing in Publication Data
Sadler, Wendy
Electricity. – (Science in your life)
537
A full catalogue record for this book is available from the British Library.

Acknowledgements
Alamy Images pp. 6 (bobo), 22 (Fogstock), 5 (Hemera Technologies), 23 (imageshop-zefa visual media uk ltd), 8 (JG Photography), 21 (Leslie Garland Picture Library), 17 (Peter Dazely); Corbis pp. 11 (Ariel Skelley), 13 (Bettman), 24 (Pete Saloutos), 16 (Sygma/Yassukovich), 12 (Tom Stewart); Corbis Royalty Free p. 14; GE Consumer & Industrial p. 9; Getty Images pp. 19, 20, 25, 29 (PhotoDisc); Harcourt Education Ltd p. 27 (Tudor Photography); Photographers Direct p. 18 (Dave Hebden); Photolibrary.com p. 4; Science Photo Library p. 26 (Peter Menzel); The Picture Source p. 15 (Terry Oakley).

Cover photograph of electricity pylons in front of an orange sunset reproduced with permission of Corbis/Lester Lefkowitz.

Every effort has been made to contact copyright holders of any material reproduced in this book. Any omissions will be rectified in subsequent printings if notice is given to the publishers.

The paper used to print this book comes from sustainable resources.

Disclaimer
All the Internet addresses (URLs) given in this book were valid at the time of going to press. However, due to the dynamic nature of the Internet, some addresses may have changed, or sites may have changed or ceased to exist since publication. While the author and publishers regret any inconvenience this may cause readers, no responsibility for any such changes can be accepted by either the author or the publishers.

An adult should supervise all of the activities in this book.

Contents

Any words appearing in the text in bold, **like this**, are explained in the glossary.

Have you used electricity today?

Have you used electricity today? Lots of the things that we do each day involve electricity. Electricity can heat things up and make things light up. It can make things move and it can even make sounds.

A fridge needs electricity to keep things cool.

Electricity in your life!

Here are some ways that we use electricity:

- keeping milk cold in a fridge
- making toast in a toaster
- watching television
- turning on a light
- playing a computer game
- travelling in a car, train, or bus
- running warm water from a tap.

How many of these have you done today? Can you think of any other things you have done that used electricity? Imagine what your life would be like without electricity!

Electricity can be switched on and off when we need it.

TURBO POWER H.D.D.

What is electricity?

Electricity is a kind of **energy**. The energy comes from tiny **particles** called **electrons**. When the electrons move along inside a wire we say that electricity is flowing.

The energy from electricity can make things glow, warm up, or move. We can also use the energy to send **signals** along a wire. For example, a computer mouse sends signals along a wire to the computer.

Wires like these can carry electricity all around buildings.

Electricity can only flow if the wires join up with no gaps. This is called an electric **circuit**. If we put a gap in the circuit, the electricity will stop flowing. If we close the gap, the electricity will flow again. These gaps that open and close are called **switches**. They turn electricity on and off.

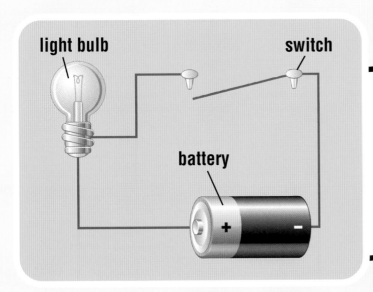

When the switch is open, there is a gap in the circuit. The electricity cannot flow, so the bulb does not light.

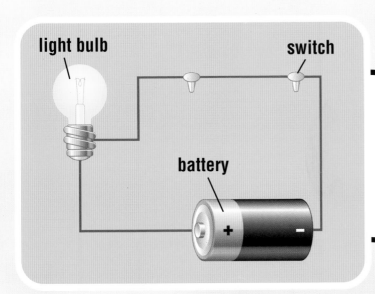

When the switch is closed, there is no gap in the circuit. The electricity can flow, so the bulb lights up.

Heating and lighting

The little **particles** of electricity (called **electrons**) move along inside wires. They push against other particles that get in the way. We call this **resistance**. All the pushing makes the electrons hot.

The red wires you see inside a toaster are hot because of the resistance in the wires. The electrons are full of energy and this makes the wires glow red.

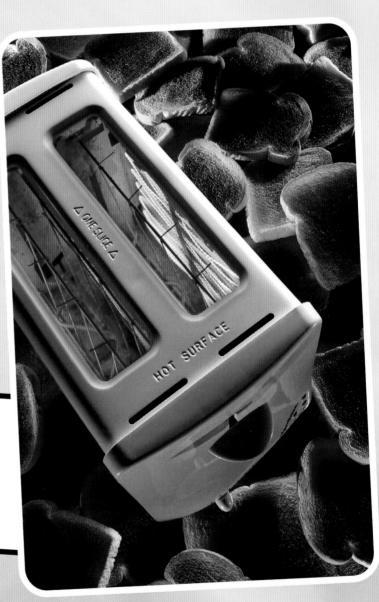

The wires inside a toaster make enough heat to turn bread into crispy toast for your breakfast!

How does electricity make light?

Inside an ordinary light bulb there is a very thin wire. This glows brightly when electricity flows through it. This wire is called a **filament**. When the filament glows it also makes a lot of heat. This heat is wasted energy because it is not used for anything.

These light bulbs makes light without heat. It is called "energy efficient". Do you have any of these bulbs at home?

Electricity and **magnets** can be used in an electric **motor** to make things move. An electric motor is made of a coil of wire and some magnets. When electricity flows in the wire it makes a **magnetic field** around the wire.

Two magnets that have the same force will push each other apart. Two magnets that have opposite forces will pull towards each other. These pushes and pulls between the magnets and the wire make the motor move.

This diagram shows how a magnet and a coil of wire can make electricity, which can be used in an electric motor.

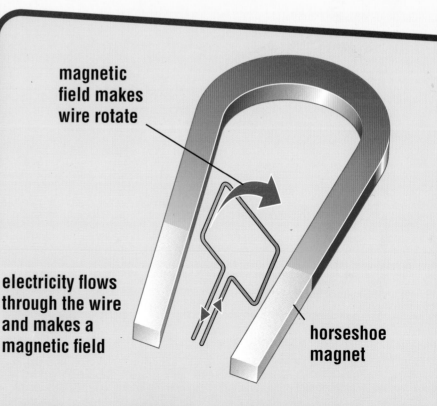

magnetic field makes wire rotate

electricity flows through the wire and makes a magnetic field

horseshoe magnet

What do we use electric motors for?

There are lots of motors all around you! They can be found inside cars, washing machines, DVD players, and computers. Most things that move when you plug them in have some kind of motor inside them.

This food mixer uses a motor. Electricity is turned into movement to spin the food.

Sending signals with electricity

Electricity can be used to send **signals** or messages. Electric **current** is a measure of how much electricity is flowing. A big electric current is a lot of electricity and a small current is less electricity.

When you speak into a telephone, the pattern of your voice is turned into a pattern of electric current. This pattern is sent along the telephone wires. At the other end, the electric current is turned back into sound so the other person can hear your voice!

Electricity helps us in many different ways every day. We would not be able to call our friends on the telephone without it!

What would happen without telephones?

How would we talk to people far away without telephones? Before telephones, people used flags and smoke signals to send messages. But this would only work over quite short distances!

This person is using flags to send a message. This is called semaphore.

A video recorder uses the same idea as the telephone. Pictures and sounds are stored on the videotape as a **magnetic** pattern. The video player reads the pattern and turns it into an electric pattern. The television turns the electric pattern back into pictures and sounds so you can enjoy your favourite film!

Electricity in action: washing machines

Before we had washing machines people had to wash all their clothes by hand. Washing machines use electricity to make the job quicker and easier.

Electricity heats up the water in the washing machine. Hot water is better at getting dirt out than cold water.

The drum inside a washing machine is the part where you put your dirty clothes. It moves around to make sure all the clothes get covered in water and washing powder. An electric **motor** turns the drum.

Electricity does many different things inside a washing machine.

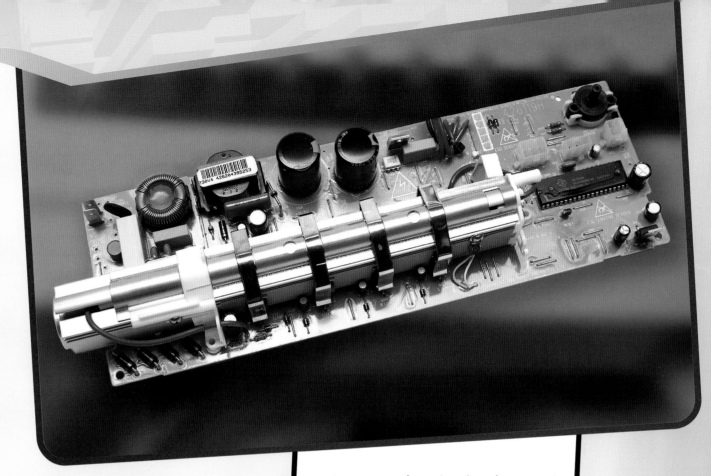

This tiny electric circuit controls a washing machine.

A valve is something that can open or close to let water flow or to stop it flowing. Electric valves are used to put in and take out water at the right times during the wash cycle.

Different clothes need different types of washing. Some need very hot water and others need colder water. An electric clock and heater control how long each part of the wash lasts and how hot the water is.

Electricity in action: cars

Electricity in your life!

Next time you are in a car, try to work out all the things that use electricity. Hint: look for anything that moves, heats up, or lights up!

A car needs an electric spark to start up its engine. This spark comes from a big, powerful battery. The battery can give out electricity for a long time because it is **rechargeable**. Energy from the engine is used to charge up the battery every time the car is used. A machine called an **alternator** turns the movement from the engine into electricity so that the battery stays charged.

If the alternator is not working properly, or the lights are left on while the engine is off, then the battery will go flat. A car will not start without electricity from the battery.

engine

The battery in a car provides the electric spark that starts the engine.

battery

Conductors and insulators

In some **materials** the **particles** that carry electricity are quite loose so they can move around easily. These materials are called **conductors**. A conductor lets electricity flow through it. Metal objects and water are both good conductors.

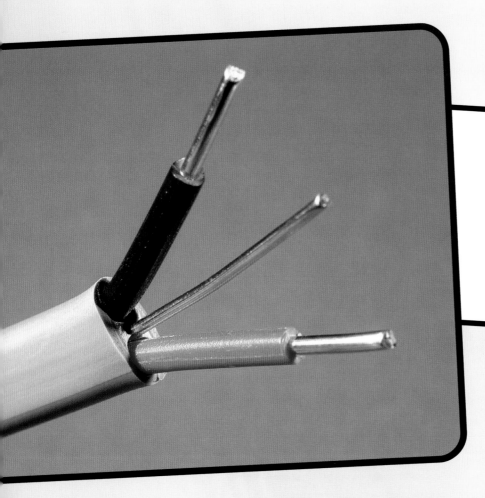

Metal wires are good conductors of electricity. They are covered in plastic to protect us from the electricity.

In other materials the particles are held tightly in one place. If you try to make them move, they will not! Because the particles do not move, electricity cannot flow. These materials are called **insulators**. Air, rubber, and plastic are all insulators.

There are some amazing materials that are called semi-conductors. These sometimes let electricity flow and sometimes do not! Computers have lots of semi-conductors inside them.

Air is an insulator. The electricity that flows through these wires will not escape because the electricity cannot flow out through the air.

Where does electricity come from?

Electricity can be made using a **generator**. A generator is a bit like a **motor**, but it does the opposite job. A motor turns electricity into movement. A generator turns movement into electricity.

A generator contains coils of wire and magnets. The moving wire or magnet makes an electric **current** flow in the wire. Wind, water, or hot steam can be used to spin the wire or magnet.

This power station uses generators to make electricity.

In a power station a fuel, such as coal, is burned to heat water. When the water boils it makes steam. Most electricity is made using hot steam to spin the wires or magnets.

Different-sized batteries can give different-sized electric currents.

We also use batteries to give us electricity. **Chemicals** inside the battery make electricity flow in the wires. Usually batteries will go flat after a while. Some batteries, such as mobile phone batteries, can be charged up again by plugging them into an electric socket.

Electricity and safety

Electricity has a lot of **energy**. It can be very dangerous and can hurt you, burn you, or even kill you. You should never put anything into an electric socket except a plug that is made for that kind of socket. All electric wires should be covered with an **insulator**, such as plastic, so that the electricity does not touch you.

Electricity is very dangerous. You should never ignore signs like these that warn of the dangers of electricity.

Water **conducts** electricity well. This means that it is not safe to have anything electrical near water or in your bathroom. Machines that use electricity and water, such as an electric shower or a washing machine, are made with lots of insulation. This keeps the water and the electricity apart.

You should not use a hairdryer in the bathroom in case it gets wet. Electricity can travel from the hairdryer, through the water, and into you.

Electricity in nature

Your body makes and uses small amounts of electricity! When you hear a sound or smell a smell, your body sends electric messages to your brain.

When you move your body using your **muscles**, your brain sends tiny electric messages that tell your muscles to move. In fact, every little action or thought **generates** tiny electric **currents** in your body.

Special machines in hospitals can take pictures of the electric currents that happen inside your brain.

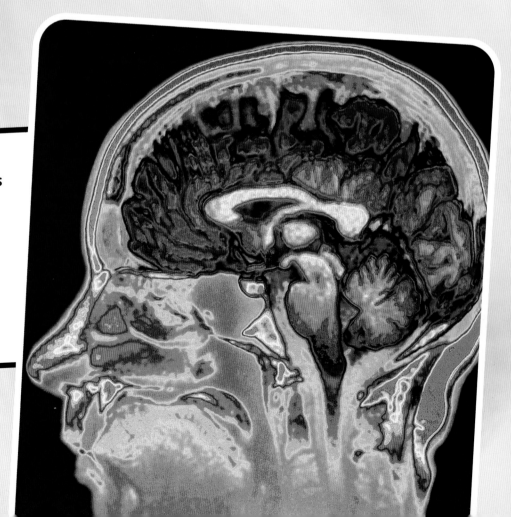

If you go to a different country you might find the plug sockets are a different shape. You need something called an **adaptor** so that you can plug your electrical things in.

Electricity is measured in **volts**. Lightning can carry a million volts of electricity!

Find out more

You can find out more about science in everyday life by talking to your teacher or parents. Your local library will also have books that can help. You will find the answers to many of your questions in this book. If you want to know more, you can use other books and the Internet.

Books to read

Discovering Science: Electricity and Magnetism, Rebecca Hunter (Raintree, 2003)
Science Answers: Electricity, Chris Cooper (Heinemann Library, 2003)
Science Files: Electricity and Magnetism, Steve Parker (Heinemann Library, 2004)

Using the Internet

Explore the Internet to find out more about electricity. Try using a search engine such as www.yahooligans or www.internet4kids.com, and type in keywords such as "battery", "**current**", and "electric **circuit**".

Glossary

adaptor object that lets you connect an electric plug into a socket that has a different shape

alternator machine that turns movement from a car engine into electricity to keep the car battery charged

chemical special substance. Everything around us is made of chemicals. Some are natural and some are man-made.

circuit when wires are joined up and there are no gaps

conductor something that lets electricity flow. Metal is a conductor.

current electricity that flows around a circuit in wires or as messages in the body

electrons tiny pieces that make electricity when they move

energy power to make things work. You need energy to get up and walk or run around.

filament thin piece of wire that gets hot and lights up inside a light bulb

generator machine that turns movement into electricity

insulator something that does not let electricity flow through it

magnet special material that can stick to other magnets, or to some metals

magnetic field area around a magnet where the force of the magnet pushes and pulls

materials something that objects are made from

motor machine that turns electricity into movement

muscles parts of the body that help us to move around

particles very tiny pieces. Everything all around you is made up of particles.

rechargeable something that can have energy put back in when it has run out

resistance when electrons push against each other in a wire

signal sign or message

switch gap in a circuit that can be used to turn electricity on and off

volts measurement of electricity